M000310783

Trader Joe's,
Take Me I'm Yours!

Joseph Cohen

For Bob, of course.

All images from the Everett Collection of Shutterstock.
Neither this book nor its author is affiliated with, associated with, authorized by, endorsed by, commissioned by or in any way officially connected to Trader Joe's, or any of its subsidiaries or affiliates. TRADER JOE'S is a registered trademark of Trader Joe's Company. The use of "Trader Joe's" in print and e-book formats and/or in any related promotional materials is strictly for illustrative purposes.

Copyright © 2018 Joseph Cohen

Do you love Trader Joe's as much as I do?

Talk about dumb questions. Of course you do. That's why you bought this book. Or why a pretty terrific friend bought it for you.

What is it about this place...this experience...this *phenomenon*? Is it the fun of discovering new things every visit? The fancy faraway flavors? The zip-a-dee-doo-dah Crew? The great prices? The free coffee. The corny signs? The buckets of beautiful flowers? The feel-good vibes?

In one word: Yup!

Like the best kind of love, Trader Joe's isn't a heart-thumping swoon at first sight. It grows on you. Visit by visit. Nibble by nibble. Pound by pound.

Something tells me my Trader Joe's journey is yours as well. So please, tag along. And if you happen to see me at your local Trader's—invariably standing in front of the cheese or chips or ice cream in a decision-making daze—I hope you'll say "hello." I can't wait to hear your Trader Joe's story, too.

Long, long ago.
Well, actually, not that long ago.

Shopping for food was such a bore.
A downright snore.

Hey, Froot Loops and Planters Mixed Nuts
were the most exciting things on the supermarket shelves.

But we just knew there had to be something better.

"Swami, what do you see in my future?"

"I see lots and lots of chocolate and flowers and something called Chuck..."

"But what does it all mean?"

"Damned if I know."

And then one never-to-be-forgotten day
we heard about Trader Joe's.

Maybe it was a pal in Cal. raving about
Trader's Peanut Butter Stuffed Pretzels...

"You eat one and then you reach for
 another one and before you know it
they're all gone!"

Might have been that superstar gushing
over Trader's incredibly cheap flowers...

"People think I'm a gazillionaire.
I'm just a humble billionaire!"

Perhaps it was Aunt Milly in Boston
drooling over the Pastrami Lox...

"The smell reminds me of your
Uncle Izzy, may he rest in peace."

Dear friends, it matters not how Trader Joe's dribbled into our freshly Q-tipped eardrums.
From that magical moment, we dreamed of the day when Trader's would open right in our own backyard.

"I'm sure they'll want me for the ribbon cutting."

And then it happened.

Ring-a-ding-ding.

Mama mia.

The hills are alive with the sound of hummus.

Yikes, so much stuff.
Where do you start?

First impressions.
What do you remember most?

All these nuts are getting me nuts.

Who thinks up these clever names?

I'm hearing bells. Are we near
a church?

Somebody out there must
love cauliflower.

I've never seen Seasoned Buffalo Ghee so cheap .
(Then again, I've never seen Seasoned Buffalo Ghee.)

Why is everbody
so darn happy?

My kid can draw better signs.

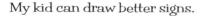

I thought Sriracha was
a Mexican folk dance.

I've never seen Chocolate-Covered Edamame so cheap.
(Then again, I've never seen Chocolate-Covered Edamame.)

Cute tee shirts on the help...forgive me, I mean the Crew.

Potatoes from France, very Francy.

Orchid plants for $12.99? I'll buy five!

What the heck is
Spatchcocked Chicken?

Greeting cards. Who knew?
I wonder if they sell stamps.

That first unforgettable visit
two hours later.

This aisle looks awfully familiar.
Yup, there are those adorable Silver Dollar Pancakes.
My kids will love 'em.
Wait, they're already in my cart.

I'm in a trance.
I'm seeing double.
I can't read another package.
My tulips are wilting.
My Mango Mini Mochi is melted mush.

Get me outta here!

By visit #three, you're on a roll.

Pork Shumai there, Unexpected Cheddar here,
Take a Hike Trail Mix 'round the bend...

Look at you, dashing through the store. You're on auto-pilot.

But wouldn't you know it.
Just when you're absolutely sure where everything is...

They move the Colossal Stuffed Olives to a whole other aisle.
Where's the Turkey Jerky? It used to be right there.
I swear the Mini Brie en Croute was right here two days ago.

As if all of this wasn't bad enough...

Holy moly, I gotta poo!
(No surprise after three cups of free coffee.)

Where's the bathroom?
Do they even have a bathroom?
This is getting serious!

Just in the nick of time, you find the bathroom.
You attend to business.
And then you make the big mistake of looking in the mirror.

Do you really look that bad? You do not!
The cans at Sing Sing have more flattering lighting.

Dear friends:
Close your eyes. Wash your hands. Resume shopping.

Without the Crew,
it's just a bunch of food.

They're our personal shoppers.
Upbeat. Hustle-bustle helpful.
How do they do it all day long?

"I'm hunting for those crispy crackers with tons of seeds that stick in my teeth and I think they're from Norway.

Crews crave cryptic clues.
Give 'em a few adjectives,
you've got your crackers.

(Don't you love the way they actually escort you
to the item you're looking for?)

What are your Crew-dentials?

Do you have favorite Crew members?
Do you remember their names (without peeking at their tags)?
Do they know *your* name?
Do you get misty eyed when you see the way they help people
who need extra assistance?

Do you pray they'll find one more package of
Apple Blossom Tarts in the back room?
(Which you'll tell everyone you baked that very morning.)

Ever wonder if they still like people at the end of the day?

Ever wonder if *you* could work at Trader Joe's?

By now, you must be
getting pretty hungry.

You can't love everything at Trader Joe's.
But when you're smitten, it's big time.

The raves go something like this:

"OMG, have you tried their Parmesan Pastry Pups'?"
"OMG, you gotta get their Coffee Blast Ice Cream."
"OMG, their Rice Pudding is so creamy and elegant."
"OMG, don't get me started on their Mango Ginger Chutney."
"OMG, the Cold Pressed Watermelon Juice is
summer in a bottle."

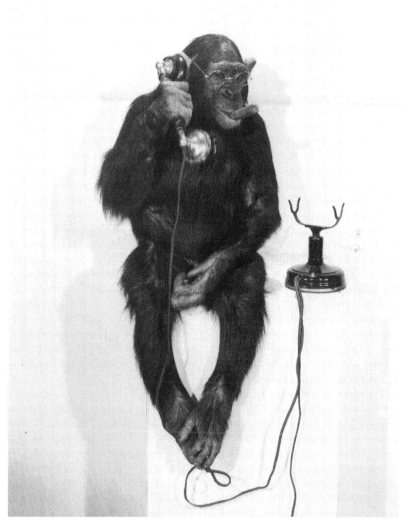

"OMG, I've never seen such magnificent bananas."

Trader Joe's can be a truly religious experience...

...most of the time.

The gripes go something like this:

"The Chicken Tenders weren't very tender."
"The Cowboy Caviar wasn't real caviar."
"The Organic Prune Juice made me gassy."
"The Cruciferous Crunch could have been a lot crunchier."
"I found a pit in the Pitted Cherries."

"There's enough salt in this stuff to melt the snow
in my driveway!"

If you don't like something at TJ's, return it!
(Of course, sometimes you have to eat a lot of something
to be really sure you don't like it. So try to save a few crumbs
or spoonfuls.)

Now you see it,
now you don't.

Life can be so cruel.

Just when you're head over heels over something at Trader Joe's, it's gone. Kaput!

The Organic Pea Soup has vanished.
"Seasonal," says Crew mate Molly.

The Red Boat Fish Sauce has sailed into the sunset.
"It always drifts back to shore," consoles Crew mate Zachary.

The Beet Hummus used to be right here.
"Beats me!" quips Crew mate Cindy.

Tip #1: Treasure the delectable memories.
Tip #2: Stock up big time.
Tip #3: Throw a hissy fit in front of the manager, aka Captain.
Tip #4: Fall in love with something new.

Time for a topic detour:
The Case of the Quivering Ears

It's truly amazing.
We can be sitting in Starbucks minding our own business
(*sorta*).
All of a sudden, our ears start to vibrate.
We're picking up a signal from clear across the room.
It's coming in loud and strong:
*"Three Layer Hummus...Pickled Popcorn...Hold the Cone...
This Fig Walks Into..."*

Our ears are smoking. They're on fire!
It's all we can do to not jump up and join the conversation.

Go for it!

Share the Love

It's our moral imperative to talk up our favorite TJ discoveries
wherever we are. Hey, we know what's good.
And if we really like something, everybody should love it, too.

Talk/yak.
Yak/talk.

Is it me, or does it seem like every chat
inevitably leads to Trader Joe's?

A scholarly no-expense-spared survey of current conversational content.

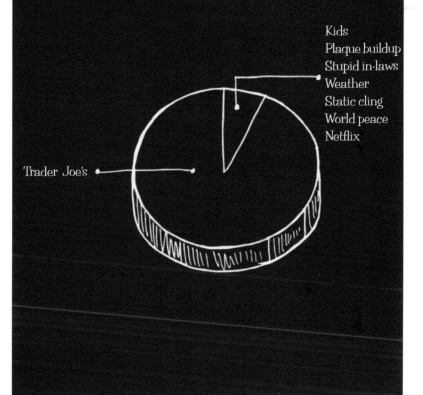

Kids
Plaque buildup
Stupid in-laws
Weather
Static cling
World peace
Netflix

Trader Joe's

But what about the friends, spouses, kids, paramours and pets who don't love Trader's like we do? Are we torturing them with our endless TJ clucking?

We must be sensitive to their feelings.

· Avoid saying Trader Joe's in their presence.
· Hand them earplugs.
· Fool 'em, make up a new name for Trader Joe's.
· Learn sign language.
· Talk about catheters for 10 minutes, and they'll be begging for Trader Joe's.

Become a semaphore savant.
(Translation : The parking lot is a zoo!)

It's back and
we can't escape it.

It's pumpkin time.

That glorious,
orange-colored,
nutmeg-scented,
everywhere-you-look,
what-will-they-think-of-next,
wake-me-up-when- it's-over
time of year
when pumpkins pump up EVERYTHING.

There's not a pumpkin left on the planet.

Hey, all of you brilliant brainstormers in Monrovia.*
Where's the pumpkin shampoo?

*Headquarters of Trader Joe's. 800 South Shamrock Avenue,
Monrovia, California

What TJ pumpkin concoctions have you tried?

Bagels
Beer
Biscotti
Butter
Cereal
Cheesecake
Chips
Chocolates
Coffee
Crackers
Cream Cheese
Croissants
Croutons
Granola
Ice Cream
Joe-Joe's
Joe-O's
Macarons
Mochi
Pancakes
Pasta
Pies
Pudding
Ravioli
Rolls
Spaghetti Sauce
Tea
Yogurt

Ho-ho-ho, Ho-hum.
When one holiday ends, a new one begins at Trader Joe's.

Trader Troopers, you've soldiered your way past Easter
Bunny Gummy Tummies and Ugly Sweater Christmas Cookie
Kits and St. Paddy Irish Bangers and Turkey & Stuffing Kettle
Chips and Cinco de Mayo Salsas and
Halloween Joe-Joe's Cookies.

If it's okay with you, let's take a break from all this
holiday cheer.
Let's make our way to the check-out line.

You've got to be kidding.
This is just the MIDDLE of the line?!

Unless you get up with the roosters,
unless you shop at the world's largest Trader Joe's,
unless you pretend you were at the head of the line but you
forgot the 10-Minute Barley and now you're back...

Get ready to wait in line.

Some people will do anything to get to the front of the line.

Sometimes we read our mail while we're doing the
check-out Cha-Cha.
Sometimes we annoy shoppers and call a friend.
Lots of times we talk to ourselves.
But here's one of our all-time favorite things...

Judging people by the items in their cart.
(Although we'd never admit that's what we're doing.)

The Calorie Counters

Fit as a fiddle—whatever that means—with their bags of Brussels Sprouts, Tuscan Kale and Baby Spinach. Wait a second, is that Trader's Icelandic Cheese Cake slyly secreted beneath this blanket of green? No wonder they're smiling!

The Ingenue

She's gonna be a star, you just know it...with her cart filled with Trader Joe's Rose Water Facial Toner, Lavender Salt Scrub, Mango Body Butter and Tea Tree Tingle Shampoo. Even when she's rich and famous, she'll still shop Trader's "Aisle of Beauty."

The Best Friend's Best Friend

It's all about Mademoiselle Maisey: Glucosamine Chondroitin for Dogs, Smoked Chicken Tenders, Salmon Jerky Treats and Mint-A-Breath Bones. Of course, if you ask Maisey, she'd be ecstatic with a heaping bowl of Trader's Mandarin Orange Chicken.

The Life of the Party
Keep your eyes on the lifeboats! He's setting sail with TJ's Petit Reserve
Pinot Noir, Fig & Olive Crisps, Goat Cheese Medallions and Trader's Five
Pound Belgium Chocolate Bar. Pray for smooth seas.

Beware the aisle of
irresistible temptations.

WARNING!!!!

You're "this close" to checking out.
Look straight ahead.
Don't even dream of glancing left and right.

Are you strong enough to resist the Siren's call:
the sweet seduction of Tahitian Vanilla Caramels
and Chewy Oatmeal Cookies and Dark Chocolate
Peanut Butter Cups
and Cocoa Batons and Chocolate Coconut Almonds and
Milk Chocolate Crisps and...

TOO LATE!!!!

Overtaken by an invisible force, your right hand reaches for
the triangular tease of Toblerone.
Your left hand grabs the Soft-Baked Snickerdoodles.
You're feeling the magnetic force of Oven-Baked Cheese Bites
and Spud Crunchies.
The Pomegranate Breath Mints look so darn cute, you grab two.

You swear this lapse of self-control will never happen again.

Sure.

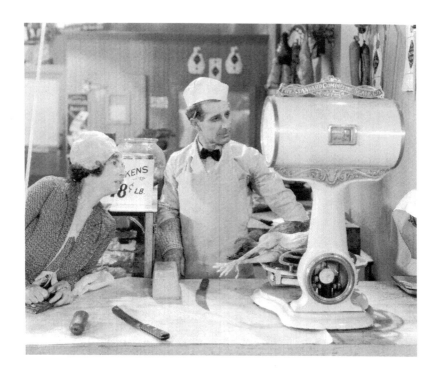

Checking out.
Chatting up.

It's time for a few moments of bonding bliss, as we proudly hand over our matched set of Trader Joe's shopping totes and start our "interrogation" with a breezy "How you doin'?"

Doesn't matter who's
checking you out.
It's always service with a smile.

We're not nosy. We're just really interested.
That's why we ask our favorite check-out questions
over and over again.

Do you like working here?
Been here long?
Do you get health insurance?
What's your favorite TJ assignment?
Do you have to pay for your tee shirts?
Are you allowed to accessorize?
Do they let you sample everything?
Have you gained weight?
What's your fave TJ food?
Tried the Scandinavian Swimmer Gummies?
What do you mean you're afraid of the water?

Do you guys ever get tired?

Congratulations,
your home just quadrupled
in value.

People love Trader Joe's for all kinds of reasons.
But here's what's really making front-page headlines:
home values are skyrocketing when there's a TJ's nearby.
(If the schools are good, too...you're sitting on a goldmine!)

Love's a personal, quirky kind of thing.
When it comes to Trader Joe's, the love-fest is limitless.

I love trying all kinds of new things at Trader Joe's.

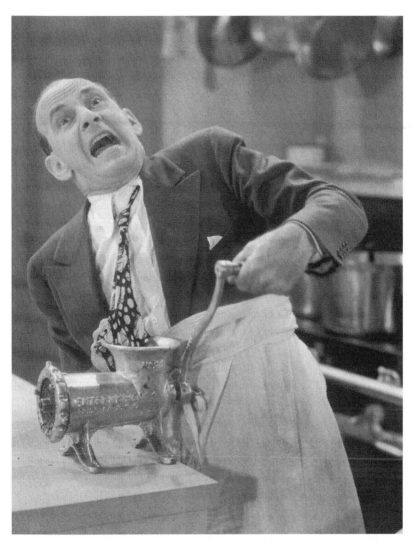

I love their prepared meals and not getting stuck in the kitchen.

I love the exquisite effervescence of their
Sparkling Pink Lemonade.

I love the serendipitous delight of bumping into old friends at Trader Joe's.

I love the hours we share reading the Fearless Flyer.

I love the notes of strawberry and tractor in their
Two Buck Chuck Cabernet.

I love buying every flower that captures my fancy.

We love the zesty zip of their Key Lime Shortbread Cookies.

I love never having to spend a bundle of money.

You're probably saying to yourself:
"I could have written this book!"

Thoughtful me, I did it for you.
So you could spend more time shopping at Trader Joe's.
But you're not off the hook.
Something tells me you've got a bundle of
nowhere-else-but-Trader Joe's
moments of your own. All itching to be shared.
Couldn't be easier.

www.TraderJoesImYours.com

@TraderJoesImYours

A Few Tidbits About Joseph Cohen

Joe ♥ Joe's. If you've gotten this far, you know that already. But there's a sweet life for Joseph Cohen beyond Trader Joe's and its endless temptations. Joseph is an award-winning copywriter, he names many of your favorite products, and he's a bestselling author with over one million books in print. The fuzzy warmth of *A Good Friend* and *I Love You Because* are flip-sided by the buzzy zing of *You Know You're Gay When* and *The Penis Book*. And now there's *Trader Joe's, Take Me I'm Yours!* Something for everyone. Indeed.

www.RaySinghPhotography.com

97682322R00061

Made in the USA
Lexington, KY
31 August 2018